Copyright © 2024 Frank Amat

All rights reserved

ISBN: 9798345504123

I dedicate this book to my family: the one I knew, the one I know, and the one I will never know

Table of Contents

	Introduction..	3
One.	The Stock Markets..	7
Two.	How Can I Invest in the Stock Markets?................	9
Three.	Advantages and Disadvantages.............................	17
Four.	The Stocks...	23
Five.	Real Estate or Stocks?...	25
Six.	The Best Financial Asset.......................................	27
Seven.	The Eighth Wonder of the World..........................	29
Eight.	Start as Soon as Possible.......................................	37
Nine.	One-Time or Recurring Purchases?.......................	39
Ten.	Invest in Businesses You Understand....................	43
Eleven.	The Language of Business.....................................	49
Twelve.	Seeking Fair Value..	57
Thirteen.	Managing Risks...	61
Fourteen.	Psychology: Your Best Ally...................................	67
Fifteen.	How to Handle a Stock Market "Crash"................	73
Sixteen.	Companies That Have Multiplied Their Wealth....	81
	Final Thoughts..	97

Disclaimer

The information, opinions, graphs, and calculations presented in this book are for informational purposes only and do not constitute investment recommendations, invitations, offers, solicitations, or financial advice. As such, they should not be relied upon for asset valuation or as a basis for making purchasing, selling, or investment decisions.

Introduction

Writing a book requires dedication, perseverance, and above all, time. A lot of time, if you truly want to deliver value to the reader, which is what I've intended from the moment I decided to write this book.

Knowing that our time is finite, scarce, and that this very scarcity is what gives it an immeasurable value (since we cannot know when we will leave this world or when our "useful" life will end), why have I dedicated part of my limited lifetime to writing this book?

Well, the reasons that have led me to write it are, essentially, the following:

1. **Sharing knowledge so that people can generate wealth.**

    In schools, institutes, and even in universities, financial knowledge to generate wealth is not taught, not even in university degrees related to the financial field.

    They teach knowledge that a student will never use. They explain historical events of little relevance. Yet, they don't offer personal finance classes, nor do they provide basic financial knowledge to generate—or maintain—personal wealth. Wealth that can help you achieve a better quality of life, make your dreams come true, or simply allow you and your family to be (more) free. Why does this happen? Do you really believe that none of our ancestors ever considered the importance, or the necessity, of including this knowledge in the school curriculum?

The fact that these financial skills are not taught in schools or high schools is not an accident. Governments and economic elites have always wanted to keep people ignorant, so they remain poor and dependent on the State. They know that financial knowledge can one day set you or your children free, which goes against their interests. They want you to die poor, despite having worked hard your entire life, so that your children are forced to follow the same path, and so on, generation after generation. This pattern has repeated itself throughout history.

2. Change public's perception of the stock markets.

Investing in real businesses, through the stock markets, is often mistakenly viewed as a speculative and, therefore, risky activity. The only real risk is not knowing what you're doing, and that holds true in any field. Of course, there is speculation in the stock market, but it's not an inherent feature of the stock market itself, but rather of some of its participants.

3. Leave a legacy of knowledge for my descendants.

Surely, when you hear "stock market," your personal risk protection sensor goes off, and that's perfectly normal, as we live in a society that promotes the idea that the stock market is risky. Indeed, investing in the stock market is not risk-free. But what in life is completely risk-free? Risk is part of everyday life. Therefore, you must accept this reality and face it responsibly if you want to participate and succeed, not just in investing but in any aspect of real life. If you expect to grow your wealth while sitting on the couch and avoiding all risks, I'm sorry to say that you will never achieve your dreams. However, if you are willing to take and manage relative risks, the stock market is a perfect mechanism for growing your wealth in the long term, as long as you know what you're doing and have developed the necessary skills to achieve it.

Businesses drive the world. They are efficient organizations that manage material and human resources to produce goods and/or services demanded by the public. Investing in businesses means participating in entrepreneurial ventures, some of which can be truly exciting.

Many people avoid investing in real businesses due to the fear of loss or failure. They believe that by not investing, they're protecting themselves from the risk of losing money. But what if I told you that not investing in businesses is actually a sure way to lose money? Do you know how much your savings have devalued over the past 5 or 10 years? How much money did you need as a child to buy candy, and how much do you need now? The constant devaluation of currency and the rising prices of goods and services caused by inflation is a reality. Inflation is a global phenomenon that leads to impoverishment; it's a hidden tax that eats away at your savings. So, what can we do to protect our savings? How can we stop the current government from eroding the hard-earned money we've accumulated through their expansionist policies that fuel inflation? Without a doubt, investing in real businesses offers the best protection against this programmed impoverishment, for the reasons I'll explain later.

I understand that the idea of "investing in businesses" can seem intimidating at first, especially if you've never done it before, and you are not familiar with the business world. That's perfectly normal; it was intimidating for me at first too. That's why I always recommend approaching it cautiously and prudently.

I hope this book gives you a new perspective on the stock market and investing in real businesses. I also hope it helps you stay focused when it comes to investing. Knowing how to distinguish what is important from what is not, and what you want from what you don't want, is nearly half the battle for success. If one day you find yourself turning down the vast majority of investment opportunities presented to you, you're likely heading in the direction that leads to success.

Finally, I hope the insights I've shared in this book help you grow your personal wealth. The legendary investor Warren E. Buffett has said, on more than one occasion, "price is what you pay; value is what you get." Well, I sincerely believe that the value you will receive from this book far exceeds the price you paid for it. I've spent many years investing and continuously learning to acquire the knowledge I'm sharing with you in this book.

However, keep in mind that this book is just a small, highly selective sample of something much larger, so I encourage you to continue reading and learning after finishing it. The journey of an investor is never-ending. In my opinion, it's worth diving into the world of investing, the long-term results may pleasantly surprise you!

1. The Stock Markets

You've probably heard or read about the stock markets. But what exactly are they? What is a stock market?

First, you should know that there isn't just one stock market; there are several across the world. The most well-known and important ones are in the United States, particularly the NYSE (New York Stock Exchange) and the NASDAQ (National Association of Securities Dealers Automated Quotations), the latter famous for its focus on technology stocks. Other notable exchanges include those in Tokyo, London, Paris, Frankfurt, and Shanghai, among others. In fact, most developed countries have at least one stock market.

The stock market is essentially a marketplace. When we go to our local market to buy food, we exchange goods; that is, we give a certain amount of money in exchange for a certain amount of food. The same thing happens in the stock market, with the only difference being that we give a certain amount of money in exchange for a specific number of securities, called "stocks" or "shares," which represent ownership in a real business. This is why stock exchanges are also known as equity markets.

However, unlike other markets, the stock market is highly organized, regulated, and supervised by public agencies. In the United States, this role is fulfilled by the SEC (Securities and Exchange Commission). It is important to note that the stock market deals in financial assets, not physical goods. Financial assets are intangible assets. Therefore, it's crucial that companies publish accurate information, as buyers and sellers depend on it for their decisions.

It's also worth noting that the stock market consists of shares or securities from companies that have voluntarily chosen to participate in this organized marketplace. These companies, at some point, decided to make their shares available for public trading. However, there are thousands and thousands of companies that do not want their shares listed on a stock exchange. Therefore, the stock market does not accurately represent the economy of the country in which it is located; it only reflects the performance of the companies that have chosen to be part of this organized market. Additionally, in an increasingly globalized world, the revenues of these companies typically do not come from a single country—usually the country of residence or establishment—but rather from multiple countries. As a result, a company's performance doesn't necessarily correlate with the performance of the country where it's based.

In conclusion, the stock market is a marketplace where buyers and sellers exchange financial assets for money. Anyone—whether an individual, a company, or an institution—can participate by buying and selling financial assets.

2. How Can I Invest in the Stock Markets?

To buy and sell listed stocks traded on the stock market, you must go through a brokerage firm or stockbroker, often referred to as a "broker".

Historically, traditional brokers charged high fees, and technological limitations made it difficult for small investors to participate on the stock market. As a result, for decades, stock trading was largely reserved for institutions, wealth managers, or high-net-worth individuals. However, recently, many low-cost brokers have emerged, operating through online platforms. Thanks to their easy, efficient, and affordable services, these platforms offer a great alternative for individuals looking to start investing. To buy stocks through a broker, you just need to open an account, transfer funds, and you can start investing.

You can invest in stocks directly by buying and selling shares that represent ownership in a company. However, you can also invest collectively with other investors through mutual funds, where management is delegated to a third-party investment company.

There are thousands of mutual funds from various management firms, each with different characteristics. Some invest only in stocks, while others focus on fixed income, or combine both stocks and fixed income investments. Some, known as ETFs, track the performance of an index, while others invest exclusively in companies from a specific sector (e.g., the energy sector) or countries.

The question that any investor should ask is: why should I invest in stocks through a mutual fund instead of directly purchasing the stocks myself? To answer this question, it's important to understand the basic characteristics of each type of investment:

➢ **Diversification**

Mutual funds invest in a wide variety of stocks across different companies and sectors, creating a diversified portfolio. This diversification minimizes the risk of losses, as poor performance in some stocks is often offset by better performance in others.

➢ **Professional Management**

Mutual funds are managed by professional financial analysts who specialize in evaluating and analyzing listed companies on the stock market. By investing in a mutual fund, you benefit from the expertise and knowledge of these professionals. However, this does not guarantee that you will achieve returns above the market average or even a positive return on your investment.

➢ **Taxes**

Mutual funds typically benefit from lower tax rates compared to the capital gains and dividend tax rates imposed on individuals. Additionally, in many countries, investments held in a mutual fund can be transferred or reinvested into other funds without incurring any tax costs, allowing for the reinvestment of accumulated earnings without immediate tax obligations. This advantage is not available to individual investors, who must pay taxes on capital gains every time they sell a stock. As a result, the amount available for reinvestment in other stocks is the net amount after deducting taxes on the gains, unlike Mutual fund transfers, where the gross amount can be reinvested.

- **Time Savings**

    Investing in individual stocks requires time and effort to research, select, and monitor the performance of the companies whose shares you've purchased. Investing through a mutual fund allows you to save both time and effort, as the research, selection, and tracking of company performance are handled by the fund managers.

However, investing in stocks through mutual funds has some disadvantages, including the following:

- **Costs**

    Mutual fund management companies charge a management fee based on the fund's average assets, regardless of whether the fund performed well or not during that year. Additionally, they may charge a performance fee, or "success fee", if the fund exceeds a set performance target. These fees are paid by the mutual fund itself, so they are already deducted from the fund's net asset value reported to investors. The amount of these fees can vary greatly depending on the fund, making them an important factor to consider when choosing a fund, as high fees can reduce your overall returns. To determine whether a fund's total fees are high or low relative to its assets, you should look at the TER (Total Expense Ratio).

    Beyond the management fees, it's important to consider the operational costs associated with managing a portfolio, such as transaction costs for buying or selling securities. Direct investment in stocks is also subject to these operational costs; however, since you are managing the investment yourself, you can control when to buy or sell, allowing you to manage these costs to some extent by, for example, following a Buy & Hold strategy (buying and holding investments long-term unless the business deteriorates).

In any case, when you invest in individual stocks, you do not pay any management fees on the assets managed, which typically results in lower overall costs.

> **Lack of Control**

When investing in a mutual fund, you have no control over the individual stocks that are bought or sold, nor can you influence the weighting of these stocks within the portfolio. You also cannot control the investment time horizon. All of these decisions are made by the fund manager, who is given full authority to act on behalf of the fund's investors.

> **Institutional Imperative**

The term 'institutional imperative' was coined by legendary investor Warren E. Buffett. He used it to describe the invisible pressure that most analysts and fund managers face, which drives them to invest in companies that are popular and well-regarded by the general public, rather than focusing on those that might offer a higher return but are less well-known. By doing so, they minimize their personal risk—the risk of being fired or demoted. If the fund they manage performs poorly but they've invested in stocks like Microsoft or Apple, no one will blame them, and they won't lose their job. However, the situation could be very different if their portfolio is made up of lesser-known companies, even if those are excellent investments in the medium or long term.

Fund managers know that their clients (investors) are generally impatient and focused on short-term results. Investors constantly evaluate the manager's performance and draw simplistic conclusions based on the fund's immediate returns. If, in a given year, the fund has losses but the broader market also declines, investors may view the poor performance as justified. However, if the market performs well and the fund underperforms, many investors are likely to conclude that the manager made poor investment choices, and they may even withdraw their money from the fund, despite the possibility that, over the medium or long term, the fund could outperform the broader market.

> **Legal Limitations**

In every country, investment fund regulations impose limits on how funds can invest. For example, there are limits on how much a fund can concentrate in a single stock, liquidity requirements for investments, and restrictions on the maximum amount of cash a fund can hold.

Additionally, there are limitations set by the fund's own investment policy (e.g. a fund that only invests in small-cap companies or in the healthcare sector). These policies further restrict the fund's ability to diversify beyond its chosen investment strategy.

> **The Snapshot**

Fund managers are often tempted to trade frequently, buying and selling stocks, to justify their fees, forgetting that their compensation depends on the returns they deliver, not on trade volume. In practice, this leads many managers to trade more actively than they might with their own personal assets, and this hyperactivity negatively affect fund returns. History has shown that achieving strong returns often requires avoiding excessive trading, as constant buying and selling generates transaction costs (brokerage and exchange fees) and may trigger capital gains taxes.

Additionally, as the fiscal year comes to a close, many managers execute trades to maintain or boost the fund's net asset value by the year-end (usually December 31). They understand how the investment industry works—returns are measured annually, from January 1 to December 31—so they focus on looking good in the year-end "snapshot." Additionally, the performance bonuses that fund managers receive are often based on the fund's annual returns, which provides an added incentive for these practices.

> **Collective Effect**

Investment funds, as collective investment vehicles, are influenced by the decisions of their participants. During challenging times, when stock prices drop and panic ensues, many investors tend to sell some or all of their shares in the fund. To meet these redemption requests, fund managers often have to sell certain stocks, sometimes against their own strategy, disrupting the investment process and incurring associated fees and taxes. As a result, the fund manager's investment decisions are influenced by investor actions, unlike with direct stock investments. As a co-investor, you may also be affected by these forced sales to cover redemptions from other participants.

In summary, you can invest in stocks either directly or through mutual funds, and each investor should assess which option best suits their profile. It's also important to note that these options are not mutually exclusive; in fact, it's very common to combine both stocks and mutual funds.

Lastly, it's worth mentioning that passive investment funds have gained popularity in recent years. Unlike actively managed funds, where decisions are made by fund managers or analysts, passive funds simply track the performance of an index. This is another alternative for investors to consider.

3. Advantages and Disadvantages

Investing in the stock market, like everything in life, has its pros and cons. In my opinion, though, the benefits far outweigh the drawbacks. Let's take a closer look:

Key **Positive Aspects**:

- **Opportunity to own a stake in leading businesses.**

    Without public stock markets, the vast majority of people wouldn't have the opportunity to invest in some of the world's top companies or promising business. Stock markets allow you to participate in business projects from anywhere in the world, partnering with talented individuals who share similar goals. This opens a world of possibilities. Aligning yourself with the best and leveraging their talent significantly increases the potential for wealth growth—while always remembering the inherent risks in any investment, public or private.

- **Attractive option for investors with limited capital**

    Small investors, commonly referred to as "retail" investors, who have modest capital, can invest in various businesses with relatively small amounts of money. Some stocks are available for as little as $10, $30, $50, or $100, making them accessible to nearly any investor.

    Additionally, while stocks are financial assets, certain ones allow you to indirectly invest in the real estate sector. Consequently, through the stock market, you can invest in real estate without needing a large initial investment.

- ➢ **Diversification and risk management.**

The stock market offers thousands of stocks from companies around the globe across various sectors and industries, making it easy to create a diversified portfolio. You can purchase shares from companies in different countries or specific sectors, along with other financial assets such as mutual funds and ETFs. In contrast, other markets, such as the real estate market, often require significant investment in a single asset, concentrating risk—where a setback could lead to considerable loss.

- ➢ **Liquidity.**

The stock market is generally an extremely liquid market. Most of the stocks traded on major exchanges worldwide receive thousands of buy and sell orders each day, making it easy and quick to exit an investment. However, it's important to note that there are also illiquid stocks with low trading volumes, so it's advisable to always check the average trading volume of each security to manage liquidity risk. Nonetheless, the liquidity risk in the stock market is likely much lower than in other markets.

- ➢ **Business disengagement.**

The stock market allows investors to hold fractional ownership in companies and share in their success without complications. Company executives manage all business operations and day-to-day issues. Shareholders only need to monitor the company's progress and wait for a return on their investment.

- ➢ **Potential for high returns**

History has shown that certain stocks can appreciate in price over decades, allowing investors to achieve returns equivalent to 5, 10, 20, or even 100 times their initial investment. The famous investor Peter Lynch coined the term "multibagger" for this type of stocks. This potential for significant growth is not available in all markets. For example, in the real estate or second-hand furniture market, achieving a return of 100 times or more the purchase price of an asset is highly unlikely, if not impossible.

➢ **Protection against inflation.**

Inflation is an economic phenomenon characterized by a general rise in prices. It acts as a hidden tax, gradually eroding the economic value of existing currency. In other words, it reduces people's purchasing power without them realizing it, since it doesn't affect the nominal value of money. Individuals may receive the same salary, but the purchasing power of their income declines due to inflation.

Where can individuals invest to protect themselves from inflation and maintain their purchasing power? While there are various alternatives, such as real estate, gold, and other precious metals, stocks have proven to be one of the best assets for hedging against inflation. This is especially true for stocks of companies that invest in or manage tangible assets, like real estate, consumer staples, or energy products, and those that can increase their prices without losing customers due to "pricing power".

➢ **Acquire a business below its market value.**

Investing in the stock market often allows individuals to buy businesses below their intrinsic value, as stock prices fluctuate with market sentiment and expectations. This phenomenon is less common in privately held businesses for two main reasons:

1. In private companies, there is no historical price chart to reference, so the buying and selling price is based only on financials, not market sentiment.

2. When an investor wants to acquire a private business whose shares are not traded on any official stock exchange, they typically don't buy a portion of the business but rather the entire company. Sellers, aware of this, often demand a premium, or markup, above the business's market value.

- **Speed of execution.**

Trading publicly listed stocks is quick and straightforward through a broker, whether online, by phone, or via an app. This sharply contrasts with buying and selling privately held businesses, which often involves lengthy negotiations.

Key **Negative Aspects**:

- **Lack of control over the business.**

As an investor, you typically do not have control over the company, unless you are the majority shareholder, which is uncommon. Consequently, your ability to make decisions or intervene in business operations is virtually non-existent.

- **Volatility.**

Stock prices fluctuate daily, and in some cases, these variations can be more pronounced and persist for extended periods. Personally, I believe that volatility is not a disadvantage; rather, it presents an opportunity for those who know how to navigate it. However, for most people, especially beginner investors, volatility is often viewed as a negative factor and a risk. This is why I include it in the disadvantages section, even though, for experienced investors, it can be a significant advantage. In other markets, this volatility may not be as visible simply because the prices of their assets are not represented in charts. But just because it is not visible doesn't mean it doesn't exist. For example, food and fuel prices fluctuate daily.

➢ **Permanent capital loss.**

The biggest risk investors face in the stock market is the potential for a permanent capital loss. However, this risk is inherent in any investment, whether in the stock market or other markets, so it is not a disadvantage unique to stocks.

Therefore, I believe that the advantages clearly outweigh the disadvantages, making it worthwhile to invest in stocks, always with caution and understanding the risks and benefits involved in each investment.

4. The Stocks

Stocks are intangible assets traded on stock markets. They are securities that represent a specific percentage of ownership in a company. Just as cash signifies ownership of a certain amount of money, stocks represent a share of a company's assets and liabilities. When you purchase shares of a company, you are not buying its warehouse or one of its vehicles; rather, you are acquiring a small portion of its assets, debts, and future economic outcomes.

Does this mean that the company's suppliers and creditors can demand payment from you for the business debts? Absolutely not. The shares you acquire, which represent ownership in the business, are part of your personal assets, not the company's. Therefore, no supplier or creditor of the company can demand any payment from you personally. Your financial liability is limited to the amount you invested in the shares, and your personal assets are protected from the company's debts.

It is crucial to understand that a share represents real ownership in a company. It is not a lottery ticket or a bingo card. From the moment one acquires a share, a set of rights is also gained. These include economic rights, such as the right to participate in the company's profits, often distributed as dividends. Additionally, there are voting rights at shareholder meetings—unless one holds "non-voting shares," which grant only economic rights. This ownership structure empowers shareholders to influence corporate decisions while benefiting from the company's success.

When individuals start a business or corporation, they issue shares to represent ownership. This means they create equity instruments that document and reflect the value of their contributions to the company, whether those contributions are in cash or non-cash forms.

Let's illustrate the process of creating shares with an example:

"Paul and Peter decide to establish a commercial brokerage company. They estimate that an initial contribution of $100,000 each is necessary to launch the business. The total capital of $200,000 is deposited into a company bank account. Each partner owns 50% of the total capital, with $100,000 belonging to Paul and the other $100,000 to Peter. The number of shares they own depends on the value they assign to each share. For instance, if the par value is $1 per share, there will be 200,000 shares, but if the par value is $10, the total number of shares will be 20,000. Regardless of the par value, the ownership structure (50% each) remains unchanged."

Consequently, shares are instruments that represent real and fractional ownership in the underlying businesses. For example, when you purchase a share of 'Alphabet,' you are acquiring a portion of its diverse business, including Google, YouTube and Google Cloud. Therefore, you should not view shares merely as assets that can be sold, similar to a piece of furniture or jewelry. Instead, understand that there are real businesses behind these shares, and their performance will directly impact the future value of the stock.

5. Real Estate or Stocks?

Most people who want to invest their savings, or part of them, tend to choose real estate over company shares. They buy an apartment, a house, or a commercial property and rent it out for monthly income. This preference is primarily driven by five reasons:

1. Real estate is a tangible asset. It can be seen and touched, which instills a sense of security in the owner, unlike stocks, which are not physical assets.

2. Buying a property and renting it out for monthly income is perceived by many people as an easy endeavor. There is a widespread but mistaken belief that specific knowledge is not necessary to invest in real estate.

3. There are no charts capturing public sentiment regarding the daily market price or value of your real estate investment. If such charts existed, many property owners would likely have sold during the 2009 real estate crisis.

4. Most people are unfamiliar with other asset classes available for investment.

5. Investors in real estate often believe, incorrectly, that it is impossible to lose money on this type of investment.

My intention is not to criticize real estate investment, as it can be very profitable with the proper knowledge. Rather, I aim to explain why, in my opinion, most people invest their savings in rental properties, rather than other assets.

Despite being the most popular form of investment, you should know that it is not the most profitable. The net return, after expenses and taxes, from a real estate investment is unlikely to exceed 6% annually. It will likely be around 4% or 5% per year, assuming the property is well-located and in high demand.

Compared to real estate, investing in stocks can yield double-digit annual returns over long periods. If you project these high annualized returns over 10, 20, or 30 years, you will see that the cumulative return can be exponentially greater than what you would achieve by investing in real estate. This is why you will never find a real estate lessor on Forbes' list of billionaires.

However, you will find individuals like Bill Gates, Jeff Bezos, Warren Buffett, Bernard Arnault, Amancio Ortega, and countless others who have multiplied their wealth through stock investments. While I mention well-known founders of iconic companies, there are, in fact, thousands of anonymous individuals who have managed to significantly increase their wealth through investments in real businesses.

6. The Best Financial Asset

Economist and mathematician Jeremy Siegel, who served as a finance professor at the Wharton School of the University of Pennsylvania, conducted an extensive study on the returns of various types of financial assets over the past two centuries (from 1801 to 2014). The results were truly astonishing.

Let's consider an example to clarify this concept. Imagine your great-great-grandfather had taken five dollars in 1801 and permanently invested them in the following assets: $1 in stocks, $1 in bonds (public or private debt), $1 in Treasury bills (short-term public debt), $1 in gold, and $1 kept in cash. According to Jeremy Siegel's study, the returns from 1801 to 2014 would have been as follows:

1) The dollar invested in stocks would have achieved an annualized return of 6.7%, adjusted for inflation. In other words, that dollar would have appreciated a millionfold over this timeframe (1801-2014), making it worth $1,033,487 by 2014.

2) The dollar invested in bonds would have earned an annualized return of 3.5%, also adjusted for inflation, growing to $1,642 in 2014.

3) The dollar invested in Treasury bills would have yielded an annualized return of 2.7%, again after inflation, reaching $275 by 2014.

4) The dollar invested in gold would have generated an annualized return of just 0.5%, adjusted for inflation, increasing to $3.12 in 2014.

5) Finally, the dollar left uninvested in cash would have experienced an annualized return of -1.4%. Consequently, by 2014, it would be worth only $0.051, meaning that over these 213 years, its value would have depreciated by approximately 95%.

Several conclusions can be drawn from this study:

The first is that stocks are the best financial asset, historically yielding the highest returns and providing the best protection against inflation. This is primarily due to a phenomenon that I will explain in detail in the following chapter.

The second conclusion is that not investing, and keeping our money in cash, has a significant cost. In fact, this study demonstrates that, contrary to popular belief, holding money in cash is riskier than investing in stocks over the long term. While it's true that investing in certain stocks can be quite risky, keeping money in cash leads to a guaranteed loss of purchasing power due to inflation.

While investing in fixed income (bonds and Treasury bills) provided better returns than cash, stock returns were nearly 630 times higher over the same period. This is largely due to something magical that happens with stocks (be sure not to miss the next chapter).

Finally, it's worth noting that gold, often considered a "safe-haven asset," does preserve the economic value of currency, and even slightly increases it (from $1 to $3.12), after adjusting for inflation, but its returns are quite modest compared to stocks. However, like bonds and Treasury bills, gold can be a valuable asset for conservative investors looking to diversify their portfolios.

7. The Eighth Wonder of the World

"Compound interest is the eighth wonder of the world. He who understands it, earns it; he who doesn't pays it."

- Albert Einstein-

Albert Einstein, one of the most prominent scientists of the 20th century, and the 1921 Nobel Prize winner in Physics, referred to compound interest as the eighth wonder of the world. Winston Churchill, who served as Prime Minister of the United Kingdom and received the Nobel Prize in Literature in 1953, claimed that compound interest is the most powerful force in the universe. Warren E. Buffett, considered one of the greatest investors of the 20th century, once stated that the most important factor behind his success as an investor was compound interest. These individuals, along with many other geniuses from our recent history, have praised the magic of compound interest, and for good reason. It is not merely a coincidence; it confirms that compound interest is a key concept in wealth generation. Understanding compound interest provides a genuine advantage over those who do not.

What is compound interest? We can define it as the interest that is added to the initial capital on which new interest is generated over time. It is the opposite of simple interest, which does not accumulate interest on the interest generated. Let's look at an example to understand it better:

Example of simple interest at 4% on an investment of $100,000 over 5 years:

Year	Investment	Interest	Gain
1	$100,000	4%	$4,000
2	$100,000	4%	$4,000
3	$100,000	4%	$4,000
4	$100,000	4%	$4,000
5	$100,000	4%	$4,000

Accumulated gain $20,000

Example of compound interest at 4% on an investment of $100,000 over 5 years:

Year	Investment	Interest	Gain
1	$100,000	4%	$4,000
2	$104,000	4%	$4,160
3	$108,160	4%	$4,326
4	$112,486	4%	$4,499
5	$116,986	4%	$4,679

Accumulated gain $21,665

Starting with the numbers used in this example—an initial investment of $100,000 over 5 years—we can see how simple interest at 4% would generate a total return of $20,000, while compound interest at 4% would yield a total return of $21,665.

The magic of compound interest lies in how the base upon which the future interest rate is applied becomes larger each time, as it accumulates the initial capital along with all the interest earned in previous years. This leads to an increasing result, and the difference in returns between simple interest and compound interest expands over the years, as shown in the previous example.

Next, we will consider a second example, using a return rate of 10% over 10 years.

Example of simple interest at 10% on an investment of $100,000 over 10 years:

Year	Investment	Interest	Gain
1	$100,000	10%	$10,000
2	$100,000	10%	$10,000
3	$100,000	10%	$10,000
4	$100,000	10%	$10,000
5	$100,000	10%	$10,000
6	$100,000	10%	$10,000
7	$100,000	10%	$10,000
8	$100,000	10%	$10,000
9	$100,000	10%	$10,000
10	$100,000	10%	$10,000

Accumulated gain $100,000

Example of compound interest at 10% on an investment of $100,000 over 10 years:

Year	Investment	Interest	Gain
1	$100,000	10%	$10,000
2	$110,000	10%	$11,000
3	$121,000	10%	$12,100
4	$133,100	10%	$13,310
5	$146,410	10%	$14,641
6	$161,051	10%	$16,105
7	$177,156	10%	$17,716
8	$194,872	10%	$19,487
9	$214,359	10%	$21,436
10	$235,795	10%	$23,579

Accumulated gain $159,374

In this second example, the investment with compound interest generated a return of $159,374, compared to the $100,000 return from the simple interest investment. This means the compound interest investment exceeded the simple interest return by 59%.

As the investment period and rate of return increase, the difference between compound and simple interest results grows larger.

You might think, "That sounds great, but a 10% annual return over a ten-year period seems unrealistic". Well, numerous investors have achieved annual returns of 10% or higher. Moreover, the S&P 500—the most well-known stock index in the world, which includes the 500 largest U.S. companies by market capitalization—delivered average annual returns close to 10% throughout the 20th century.

To understand the role of compound interest in the world of investing, and why Albert Einstein called it the "eighth wonder of the world", it is essential to first grasp the nature of various types of investments:

- **Fixed-Income Investment**

    Investing in fixed income means acquiring debt issued by a third party, either by a government (treasury bills, bonds, or notes) or by a private company (corporate debt). The bondholder acquires debt securities in exchange for lending money to the debt issuer. This money must be repaid to the bondholder after a specified period. In compensation for lending this money, the bondholder receives a fixed annual payment, known as the "coupon.", which is based on an agreed interest rate on the principal amount.

    The debt issuer promises to repay the initial capital to the bondholder, along with the agreed-upon fixed annual return. This fixed annual return is calculated by applying a specific interest rate to the initial capital, without taking into account any returns from previous periods.

Therefore, the return on investment is based on simple interest.

- **Bank Deposit (Fixed-Term Deposit)**

The return on these deposits is calculated by applying an agreed interest rate to the initial capital, without taking into account any interest earned in previous periods. Therefore, the return is also based on the simple interest system.

- **Equity Investments (Stocks)**

Unlike fixed income investments and term deposits, equity investments involve acquiring fractional ownership in a real business. Therefore, there is no guarantee of repaying or returning the initial capital from the issuer of the shares. In this case, the return on investment is not predetermined by the counterparty in the transaction, but is instead determined by the performance of the underlying business in which a stake has been acquired.

Let's assume the business is performing well, generating profits, and growing year after year. In this case, the company's owners can choose to either reinvest the profits into the business or distribute them to shareholders. If they choose the first option, future profits are likely to grow, unless the reinvestment proves unsuccessful. First-year profits can be used to acquire income-generating assets, likely increasing second-year profits. Assume that in the second year, the company decides once again to reinvest its profits. This reinvestment allows the acquisition of new assets, increasing profits further in the third year compared to the first and second. If we project this reinvestment process over 10 years, we will see that the earnings per share in the tenth year are exponentially higher than in the first year, and this is because the profits generated over this period have been built upon an increasingly larger asset base.

Assume a company generates an annual return of 10% on its initial asset value of $10,000 over 10 years. And in each of these years, the company reinvests all annual returns into the business. Look to the following table for a simulation of this exercise.

Year	Balance	Rate (%)	Gain
1	$10,000	10	$1,000
2	$11,000	10	$1,100
3	$12,100	10	$1,210
4	$13,310	10	$1,331
5	$14,641	10	$1,464
6	$16,105	10	$1,611
7	$17,716	10	$1,772
8	$19,487	10	$1,949
9	$21,436	10	$2,144
10	$23,579	10	$2,358

Accumulated gain $15,937

We can observe that the annual return earned in the tenth year ($2,358) is significantly higher than the first-year return ($1,000), and this is due to compound interest, even though the rate of return remains constant (10%). If this were a government bond instead of a stock, the annual return in the tenth year would have been identical to the first year ($1,000), and the total accumulated return wouldn't have been $15,937, but rather $10,000.

Consequently, the effect of compound interest, which allows for exponential growth in investment returns, can only occur in equity investments (stocks). This applies as long as the investment is in profitable companies that reinvest their earnings, fully or partially, back into the business, maintaining or exceeding the current level of capital efficiency. The higher the rate of profit reinvestment, the greater the results produced by compound interest.

Due to the power of this "eighth wonder of the world," equity investments have consistently been the asset class that has generated the highest returns on invested capital over the past 200 years, far surpassing other financial assets such as fixed income, gold, and cash, as discussed in the previous chapter.

8. Start as soon as possible

Why is it important to start investing as soon as possible?

Let's consider two investors: Mark and Julia. The first, Mark, began investing at the age of 20, thanks to a small amount of capital he received from his grandfather ($10,000). He invested the $10,000 in a U.S. index fund, and since then, he has made annual contributions of $1,200 to the same fund. By the time he turns 65, his investment will have achieved an annualized return of 10%.

On the other hand, Julia started investing at the age of 35, with an initial capital of $20,000 that she saved from her career as a lawyer. She invested the $20,000 in the same U.S. index fund as Mark, and has made annual contributions of $2,400. By the time she turns 65, her investment will have also achieved an annualized return of 10%.

Which of the two do you think will have accumulated more wealth by the time they turn 65? Well, you might be surprised by the following results:

	Initial capital	Annual contribution	Annual return	Initial age	Final age	Final Capital
Mark	10.000	1.200	10%	20	65	1.677.859
Julia	20.000	2.400	10%	35	65	783.252

Despite the fact that Julia started with a larger initial capital than Mark ($20,000 compared to $10,000) and has doubled the annual contributions to the index ($2,400 compared to $1,200), she ended up with a total return that is less than half of Mark's total return ($783,252 compared to $1,677,859).

In fact, Julia has invested a total of $92,000, while Mark has invested only $64,000. Consequently, despite Julia investing $28,000 more than Mark, by the time they turn 65, Mark will have earned $894,607 more than Julia. An incredible difference!

What's the secret? It lies in the number of years in which the initial capital, along with the additional annual contributions, compounds at an annualized rate of 10%. The longer the investment period, the greater the effect of compound interest.

Therefore, if you want to invest, start as early as possible!

9. One-Time or Recurring Purchases?

As an investor, it's important to have a strategy or philosophy that guides your decision on when to invest.

Research has shown that investors who make periodic purchases (monthly or quarterly) achieve higher long-term returns compared to those who make lump-sum or random purchases. This makes sense given the volatile nature of the market. Stock prices fluctuate daily due to changes in supply and demand, and they are also affected by economic cycles. There are times of euphoria when financial assets are overvalued, and other times of widespread pessimism when they are undervalued. As a result, periodic investments align with the market price curve, allowing you to achieve a favorable average purchase price. Purchases made during euphoric times ("expensive buys") are balanced by those made during periods of pessimism ("cheap buys"). On the other hand, lump-sum investments are subject to the market conditions at the time of purchase. For example, if you have $10,000 and invest it all at once during a market upswing, you may be acquiring an overvalued asset, which could lead to modest—or even negative—returns on your investment.

Imagine that your annual investment budget is $3,600. You can either make periodic contributions to an investment fund at a rate of $300 per month, or make a single annual contribution of $3,600. It's the year 2020, and you decide to make a one-time contribution of $3,600 in February. Just one month later, a global state of emergency is declared due to the COVID-19 virus, one of the deadliest pandemics of the century. Stock markets crash, with some assets falling by 30%, 40%, or even 50%. Your lump-sum investment from February would have plummeted, and most likely, would not have recovered by the end of 2020. In contrast, if you had opted for monthly contributions, the purchases made in January and February 2020 would have been balanced by those made from March to December of the same year. Consequently, you would have achieved higher returns through periodic investing.

It's true that the scenario would have been completely different if you had made the lump-sum investment in March 2020, after the markets had crashed, as the returns then would have surpassed those from periodic investing. We know that there are always exceptions to the general rule.

However, the key takeaway is that, in the vast majority of cases, periodic investing generates higher long-term returns compared to lump-sum investments.

Additionally, periodic investing is a systematic approach that saves the investor time, as you don't have to constantly evaluate the ideal moment to invest.

Finally, I want to share some knowledge that will save you dozens, or even hundreds, of hours by avoiding a practice that has been tested over the past two hundred years and proven entirely futile. I'm referring to the attempt to predict stock price movements to identify the perfect time to invest. This practice, known as "market timing," is still used by investors who believe they have the ability to predict the future. They are completely mistaken; no one has that ability, no matter how much some may believe they do. Thus, there are two types of investors: those who know they don't have that ability, and those who don't yet realize they don't have it.

The best capital managers in the world, those who have achieved or are achieving double-digit annual returns over decades, such as Warren Buffett, Charlie Munger, Peter Lynch, and Terry Smith, to name a few, have repeatedly stated that "market timing" is of no use.

Likewise, history has shown us that stock price movements do not follow a linear path. In line with this, history has also demonstrated that if you engage in "market timing" and miss out on the best days (those when stocks experience the greatest appreciation), your annual returns will be significantly lower than those of another investor who remained invested throughout the year.

Consequently, if you decide to practice "market timing" and succeed in a particular trade, be aware of how lucky you were. Many investors attribute this success to their ability to predict the future, which often becomes the seed of their eventual failure as investors.

10. Invest in Businesses You Understand

One of the best pieces of advice from legendary investor Warren Buffett for achieving success in investing is to only invest in companies that fall within your circle of competence. In other words, invest in businesses and industries whose operations you fully understand. It doesn't matter how big your circle is, what matters is that it's well-defined and, most importantly, that you invest within it. Personally, I couldn't agree more with this principle.

Why is it so important to understand how the business and the sector in which it operates work? Well, understanding these aspects allows us to better interpret financial and accounting statements, and it enables us to assess key factors more reliably and confidently. These factors include, for example, the recurrence of cash flows, the business's growth potential, any competitive advantages it may have, and whether the goods and/or services offered will have strong demand in the future, among others.

First, one must define their own circle of competence. That is, identify which businesses you understand and which you don't, without confusing "understanding" with "knowing," even though, in some cases, you may both understand and know a business. For instance, you may know companies like Nintendo or Sony because you're a video game enthusiast, but that doesn't mean you understand how their business model works. However, you might understand the business model of a regional bank in Oklahoma, even if you've never visited its offices. Therefore, different scenarios can arise:

Scenario 1: You understand how the business works, and you are familiar with the goods and/or services it offers.

This scenario represents the ideal situation for making a successful investment, as you not only understand how the business operates but have also been a user or consumer of the goods and/or services it offers. This allows you to reliably assess the quality-to-price ratio of those products and/or services. Your familiarity with the business and its products enables you to make a better forecast of the company's future performance. For example, this situation can occur with businesses like Coca-Cola or McDonald's, whose operations are easy to understand, and whose products are well-known worldwide.

Scenario 2: You understand how the business works, but you are not familiar with the goods and/or services it offers.

If you've spent your entire career working in the hospitality and restaurant industry, you most likely understand how a hotel or restaurant operates. You know the typical margins in the sector, the level of debt, and the recurrence of revenue, among other factors. Therefore, you can objectively assess the fundamentals of an unfamiliar hospitality business, likely with greater reliability than someone who has never worked in the industry. In other cases, your understanding of the business may come from the fact that your family owns a similar business in the same sector, from studying the subject, or perhaps from dedicating countless hours to reading books, biographies, and interviews with people who have extensive experience in the field. Whatever the reason for your understanding of the business model, what truly matters is being humble and honest with yourself in verifying that this understanding is real and not just a desire to "want to understand." Otherwise, you'd only be fooling yourself, and you know who would ultimately suffer the consequences.

This situation is not as ideal as the first, since knowledge of the product or service is an important factor. It still allows you to invest in businesses that fall within your circle of competence.

Scenario 3: You don't understand how the business works, but you are familiar with the goods and/or services it offers.

I'm sure that at some point you've consumed goods or services from companies whose business model lies outside your area of expertise. In my case, aside from the video game companies mentioned earlier, I could include in this group, at the very least, companies in the pharmaceutical and biotech sectors (Pfizer, AstraZeneca, Bayer, Vertex, Amgen, etc.), companies in the technology sector (Intel, Dell, Cisco, Adobe, Oracle, etc.), and companies in the semiconductor sector (ASML, TSMC, etc.), to name a few examples.

Some of these companies are of high quality, and their stock prices have delivered great returns to shareholders. However, my lack of understanding of the specific characteristics of their business and the industry they operate in prevents me from investing in them, even though I know their products. It's not enough to know that Company X makes memory chips or that Company Y holds the patent for one of the best prostate cancer drugs. Knowledge of the business and its industry needs to be much deeper to have some level of control over the investment. Personally, I've concluded that certain sectors fall outside my circle of competence, and this has been very helpful, as it has significantly reduced the universe of stocks I consider for investment, as well as the time I spend on company selection.

Scenario 4: You don't understand how the business works, nor are you familiar with the goods and/or services it offers.

Who invests in stocks representing a business outside their competence, offering goods and/or services they are unfamiliar with? Surprisingly, it's a very common practice, even among professional managers.

There are thousands of investors buying and selling shares of companies in highly specialized sectors such as biotechnology, robotics, artificial intelligence, semiconductors, IT services, specialized medical equipment supply, nuclear energy, renewable energy, and more. These investors not only lack knowledge the goods and/or services offered by these companies, but they also don't understand the processes and mechanisms behind how the business operates, or the characteristics of the market in which they compete. Why do they do it? While there may be various reasons, it's quite common for investors to act on information they've heard suggesting that Company "X"'s stock is expected to rise in the coming days or weeks. This is typically speculative behavior and, in most cases, it's the perfect recipe for losing money on a large scale.

Once you've defined your circle of competence, you must do something even more important: always invest within that circle. Believe me, my experience has shown me that adhering to this principle is far more challenging than you might think right now.

Many professional managers fail to adhere to this principle, despite identifying as advocates of "value investing" and admirers of Warren Buffett. In practice, their actions do not align with their stated beliefs or, at the very least, with their public declarations. This inconsistency can often be attributed to the effects of what is known as the "institutional imperative." Put simply, it involves buying what's expected, rather than what you genuinely believe in, to match the market's performance and thereby safeguard your position as a portfolio manager. It's one thing if your fund loses 20 percent of its value in line with a broader market downturn, but quite another if it loses 20 percent because you invested in companies you understand, yet are less well-known to the public. In the latter case, you risk being replaced by a manager who is perceived as more aligned with the market.

Failure to comply with the maxim "always invest within your circle of competence" can also stem from an imprecise or flawed definition of what that circle actually is. In other words, you might be fully convinced that you are investing in businesses you understand and know, when in reality, your knowledge of the business or industry is insufficient. Your desire to know more than you actually do (illusion), or the false belief that you truly understand the business or sector (ego), are factors that can lead to this misstep.

The legendary investor Peter Lynch has consistently argued that individual investors can succeed in the world of investing, sometimes even more so than professional investors, as long as they focus on investing in products or services they know and understand. Although Lynch tends to emphasize familiarity with the product or service as a consumer or user, in his investment examples, he has always referenced businesses that are simple to understand, such as restaurants or beauty products. This means that beyond knowing the product or service, the individual investor must also understand how the business itself operates.

In conclusion, investing in businesses you understand and that offer goods or services with which you're familiar, is one of the best pieces of investment advice ever given. The investing community tends to undervalue this advice and often overlooks it in practice, likely because, at first glance, it appears to be an easy and unimportant rule, when in reality, it's quite the opposite.

11. The Language of Business

Accounting is the language of business. Financial information provides a clear picture of a company's health and offers insights into how its management team is running the business. Does this mean that in order to succeed as an investor, you must be an expert in accounting and finance? Absolutely not. Some of the greatest investors in history hold degrees in Law, Engineering, Mathematics, History, and other fields. However, it is important to acquire basic knowledge of accounting and finance so that you can analyze a business's key metrics. Remember, investing is not about buying pieces of paper or lottery tickets; it's about purchasing a real business that has employees and generates cash flows from selling goods and/or services.

There are dozens, if not hundreds, of books on accounting and finance, so it's impossible to compress all the knowledge I would like to share with you into this chapter. Therefore, I've selected a few basic concepts that, in my opinion, everyone who wants to invest successfully in real businesses should know. And I believe the best way to convey these concepts is through an example.

"The Ice Cream Shop"

Imagine you decide to open an ice cream shop. You have $30,000 saved up, but you've estimated that you'll need $100,000 to start the business, so you take out a $70,000 loan from the bank.

Once the business is up and running, you start selling ice cream at a price of $4 per cone. These $4 are recorded as accounting **revenue**.

However, in order to make the ice cream, you had to buy ingredients that cost, on average, $1.80 per cone. So, for each ice cream sold, you're making a **gross profit** of $2.20 ($4 - $1.8), which represents 55% of the revenue ($2.2/$4). This percentage is known as the **gross profit margin**, a key financial metric in investing. It tells us whether the company has, or could potentially have, a competitive advantage compared to other businesses in the same sector. It can also indicate whether the margin is in line with the industry average, or even below it.

To sell the ice cream, you don't just need the raw materials used to make them, you also need a physical location, for which you pay rent. Additionally, you'll need to buy or lease equipment to produce and store the ice cream, cover utility bills like electricity and water, pay employees, and hire an accountant to handle taxes, social security contributions, and other legal obligations. All of these general administrative expenses are deducted from the gross profit, resulting in the **operating profit**, or the profit generated by running the business. Let's assume this operating profit represents 37% of total revenue (i.e., $1.48 per ice cream sold). This percentage, known as the **operating profit margin**, measures the profitability of the business operations.

Next, to determine the final profit for the year, known as **net profit**, you will need to add or subtract financial income and expenses (in this example, the interest expense related to the $70,000 bank loan), as well as deduct corporate tax (the portion of your profit taken by your unwanted partner, the tax authorities). Let's assume the net profit represents 25% of total revenue ($1 for each ice cream sold). This percentage is known as the **net profit margin**.

Below is what your business's income statement would look like for a typical fiscal year:

Gross Revenue	83,333
Cost of Goods Sold	(37,500)
Gross profit	45,833
Gross Profit Margin	*55%*
General Expenses	(15,000)
Operating Profit	30,833
Operating Profit Margin	*37%*
Financial Expenses	(1,000)
Corporate Tax	(8,950)
Net Profit	20,883
Net Profit Margin	*25%*

The net profit earned during the year ($20,883) represents almost 70% of the capital you personally invested ($20,883 / $30,000). This percentage is known as the **return on equity (ROE)**.

At the same time, this $20,883 represents 20.88% of the total capital invested in the business ($20,883 / $100,000), which includes both the $30,000 you personally invested and the $70,000 borrowed from the bank. This 20.88% is the **return on invested capital (ROIC)**. Both of these metrics, ROE and ROIC, measure the business's efficiency.

After closing the fiscal year, as the sole owner, you must decide what to do with the $20,883 in net profit. You have the following options, which can be combined:

1) Pay yourself a dividend, meaning you take the $20,883, since you are the sole owner.
2) Reduce the bank debt.
3) Reinvest it in the business.

In the end, you decide to pay yourself a $10,000 dividend and reinvest the remaining $10,883 back into the business.

Your neighbor, who has noticed how well your ice cream shop is doing, decides to open one too. Like you, he invests $100,000 in the business, borrowing the full amount from his parents at a 0% interest rate.

The income statement for his business, for a typical year, would be as follows:

Gross Revenue	**102,500**
Cost of Goods Sold	(61,500)
Gross profit	**41,000**
Gross Profit Margin	*40%*
General Expenses	(30,750)
Operating Profit	**10,250**
Operating Profit Margin	*10%*
Financial Expenses	0
Corporate Tax	(3,075)
Net Profit	**7,175**
Net Profit Margin	*7,00%*

In his case, the net profit represents only 7% of the total capital invested in the business ($7,175/$100,000), which is the return on invested capital (ROIC).

After completing the fiscal year, your neighbor decides to reinvest all of the net profit back into the business, in an effort to improve future results.

Analysis:

1) Your neighbor's ice cream shop has generated higher gross revenue than yours because he sold more ice creams, achieving a higher sales volume.

2) However, since your neighbor sells his ice creams at a lower price than yours, the gross profit margin per ice cream sold is lower compared to what you've achieved at your shop (40% vs. 55%). Therefore, despite generating higher gross revenue, his shop's gross profit is lower than

yours.

3) The cost of raw materials needed to make an ice cream is the same for both businesses (you both buy from the same suppliers). Consequently, the difference in gross profit margin is primarily due to the difference in the selling price of the ice cream.

This reduction in gross profit margin affects the other margins (operating and net profit margins) as well. In other words, it triggers a cascading effect, as illustrated in the following theoretical example:

COMPANY A		COMPANY B	
Gross Revenue	83,333	Gross Revenue	83,333
Cost of Goods Sold	(37,500)	Cost of Goods Sold	(45,000)
Gross profit	**45,833**	**Gross profit**	**38,333**
Gross Profit Margin	*55%*	*Gross Profit Margin*	*46%*
General Expenses	(20,000)	General Expenses	(20,000)
Operating Profit	**25,833**	**Operating Profit**	**18,333**
Operating Profit Margin	*31%*	*Operating Profit Margin*	*22%*
Financial Expenses	(1,000)	Financial Expenses	(1,000)
Corporate Tax	(7,500)	Corporate Tax	(5,200)
Net Profit	**17,333**	**Net Profit**	**12,133**
Net Profit Margin	*21%*	*Net Profit Margin*	*15%*

4) The general expenses for your neighbor's ice cream shop account for 30% of his gross revenue, while in your case, the general expenses only represent 18% of gross revenue. This is mainly because your neighbor has rented a larger space, hired more employees, and spent more on advertising.

5) On the other hand, since you financed part of your investment through a bank loan, your business incurred a capital cost of $1,000. In contrast, your neighbor has had no capital cost, as he financed his business entirely with personal and family resources.

6) In terms of taxes, both businesses are subject to a corporate tax rate of 30%, so there is no difference here.

7) In your case, you decided to reinvest 52% of the net profit obtained, while your neighbor chose to reinvest the entire net profit. Although your neighbor has opted to reinvest a higher percentage of the net profit, your reinvestment is greater in absolute terms ($10,883 vs. $7,175).

However, what's truly important is not what I explained in the previous paragraph (which is also important), but rather what I will tell you next: there is a significant difference between the return on invested capital (ROIC) generated by your neighbor's business (7%) and the return generated by your business (20.88%). This means your business is more profitable and more efficient, as it achieves a higher return for every dollar invested. In short, your business is of higher quality.

In the short term, this difference may not have much impact. However, in the long term, it is pure dynamite. It is the "yeast" that can lead to a total disparity in the valuation of both businesses. Why? Because, given the circumstances, and assuming that both of you choose to reinvest all the net profit obtained in the business, your business will generate a return of $2,272 on the reinvested profit ($10,883 * 20.88%) in the next period, while your neighbor's business will yield a return of $502 on the reinvested profit ($7,175 * 7%).

Assuming both of you were reinvesting the same amount ($7,175), your business would generate $1,498, compared to the $502 earned by your neighbor's ice cream shop. If you run a simulation, repeating this process 20 or 30 times, you will understand why I say that the difference in ROIC is pure dynamite.

Evidently, the ROIC of both businesses will fluctuate over a period of 20 to 30 years. Additionally, other factors may affect the long-term total return on investment, such as business growth, both in terms of revenue and profits.

Conclusion:

If you had to invest your money in one of the two businesses, which one would you choose? Your neighbor's ice cream shop sells more ice creams than yours, but its return on invested capital is significantly lower than what your ice cream shop achieves. While it's true that your neighbor has invested more money in advertising, which could lead to higher sales in the future, this will not improve the gross profit margin on each ice cream sold (unless their growth leads to a monopoly or oligopoly, which is unlikely, as the ice cream market is highly fragmented and has low barriers to entry). Therefore, if I had to choose, I would opt to invest in your ice cream shop because it's a higher-quality business through which I could potentially achieve exponentially greater returns than your neighbor's (this is not a buy recommendation!).

12. Seeking Fair Value

Understanding how the businesses you invest in operate, knowing the products or services they offer, and having a basic grasp of accounting and finance to assess their financial health are key factors in making sound investment decisions, as I've discussed in previous chapters. However, these factors won't get you very far if you overpay for the business you're looking to buy. If you pay too much, you might end up with a mediocre or negative return, even on a fantastic business. Don't believe me? Just ask Microsoft shareholders from 1999, who had to wait about 16 years for the stock price to recover and surpass their initial purchase price—despite the fact that it's undeniably one of the best companies in the world.

Are Nike shoes high quality? Absolutely. But would you pay $6,000 for a pair? Of course not! The same principle applies to investing: no matter how good the quality of a product or service is, everything has a fair price.

In general, we can say that the higher the quality of a product or service, the more we're willing to pay for it—but there's a limit. That's why it's crucial to determine the price range the market is willing to pay for a given business.

In the stock market, however, we observe two peculiar phenomena that don't occur in other markets.

First, most buyers don't seek discounted stocks or bargains; instead, they tend to gravitate toward the more expensive ones. In other words, they buy the stocks that are trendy, the "hot" ones, even if it means paying a premium. In any other market, it's the opposite: people rush to grab deals and discounts, and no one in their right mind would pay $6,000 for a pair of Nike shoes that are actually worth $100 (or $60 on Black Friday). But in the stock market, the reverse often happens. Investors are attracted to those Nike shoes when they're priced at $6,000, yet they completely overlook them when they're $100. If it's Black Friday and they're marked down to $60, they practically disdain them. The instinct to fit in with the crowd, a basic survival mechanism, can override sound judgment and sometimes even common sense.

The second phenomenon, equally strange, is that the average stock buyer often doesn't know what price they're paying for their stake in a business. They know they're spending $1,000 or $4,000 to buy a handful of shares, but many don't know if they're paying a fair or inflated price for the ownership they're acquiring. People take time and effort to research whether they're getting a good deal on a microwave, or a washing machine, yet they'll throw $10,000 into shares of a company they know little about, based on something they heard on the news about how the stock will rise in the coming months. Excessive ambition and impatience cloud the investor's mind, leading to this behavior.

Therefore, the stock market is a place where a significant number of participants tend to overpay for the assets they buy, either because they're snapping up trendy, overhyped stocks, or because they're investing without properly assessing the underlying business they're purchasing. This situation creates a world of opportunity for investors who do care about valuing the businesses they acquire and who can avoid the "hot" stocks. Thanks to these two phenomena, they can often buy quality businesses at a fair price, or even at a bargain.

Valuing companies is a subject that could fill an entire book, so I won't go into too much detail here. However, it's essential to keep the following in mind:

- The price of a stock should be analyzed in relation to the underlying business's financial metrics, as well as future projections. What are the company's current earnings per share, and where might they go in the future? What kind of free cash flow per share will this business generate? How long would it take to recoup my investment if profits stay consistent? Ten years from now, will this business be worth more, considering its history of revenue and earnings, the quality of its products or services, and the trends in the industry it operates in?

- A stock's price is also influenced by the broader macroeconomic environment, including factors like inflation, recessions, interest rates, and the stages of the economic cycle. So, when evaluating a stock's price, try to identify where you are in the economic cycle. This will help you determine if the price may be inflated or undervalued and allow you to make the necessary valuation adjustments.

- A stock's price is ultimately driven by human intervention, reflected in supply and demand. The intersection of these two forces determines the stock's current price. As supply and demand levels fluctuate daily, so does the price. However, investor sentiment and expectations about the future of a business don't always align with the company's true worth. This often creates a gap between the business's real value (known as "intrinsic value") and its market price. The investor's job is to buy the stock when its market price is below the intrinsic value of the underlying business, allowing for a margin of safety.

- The best time to buy shares of a company is when their market price is below the intrinsic value of the business. However, history has shown that if the business is growing and of high quality, you can still pay a fair price and achieve great long-term returns.

- In any case, it's important not to overpay for any business, as history also shows that high future expectations often lead to great disappointments.

- As fund manager Howard Marks put it, "there is no asset so good that it can't be overpriced and become a bad investment, and very few assets are so bad that they can't be underpriced and become a good investment." What Marks meant by this is that no matter how good a business is, you must always consider the price you're paying for it. In my opinion, Marks is right in the short and medium term. However, over the long term, it will be the quality of the business and its growth, not the price you paid, that will determine the return on your investment.

Many stocks are sold at "bargain" prices. As an investor, your task is to analyze them and determine whether you're looking at a real opportunity (a good business temporarily undervalued) or a poor business whose future prospects guarantee that its shares will be worth even less down the line (beware of these situations, known as "value traps", as many investors fall into this mistake).

13. Managing Risks

"Rule No. 1: Never lose money. Rule No. 2: Never forget Rule No. 1."
- Warren E. Buffett-

This famous quote from Warren Buffett, the legendary investor, serves as a reminder that the primary goal of investing is to preserve the capital you are using. If you lose that capital, you'll have to start all over again. The hard-earned savings from months or even years of work will have been wasted, and all your efforts to accumulate those funds will have been for nothing. This is why it's crucial to invest with caution, ensuring effective risk management, because every investment carries some degree of risk.

Moreover, remember that due to simple arithmetic, losses have a greater impact than gains. For example, if a stock's price drops by 33.33%, it will need to rise by 50% just to return to its original price. Therefore, it is very difficult to succeed in the world of investing without properly managing the risks associated with your investments.

Below, I'll outline what I believe are the key risks that any stock investor should keep an eye on:

- **Market Risk:** This is the risk of experiencing a permanent loss in value due to changes or fluctuations in stock prices.

    In my view, the temporary loss of value caused by price volatility does not constitute market risk, although certain investors (particularly institutional ones) may consider it as such. Temporary price declines in an asset are inherent to the nature of any market, as price fluctuations occur in response to supply and demand dynamics or other macroeconomic factors (wars, pandemics, etc.). The volatility in an asset's price merely reflects the sentiment or perception of the investing community about that asset at a specific point in time. However, the actual value of the asset is not determined by what investors think or believe at any given moment; it is only affected by the real performance of the underlying business.

- **Currency Risk:** This risk only comes into play when you invest using a currency different from your local or reference currency. It refers to the risk of incurring losses due to fluctuations between your reference currency and the currency used for the investment. Most stocks are listed in only one market and traded in a single currency, so if you want to invest in them, you will first need to exchange your local currency for the trading currency of the asset. In these cases, currency risk must be considered in addition to market risk.

- **Liquidity Risk:** This is the risk of being unable to exit a position within your desired timeframe or at your intended price, due to the low trading volume of a particular stock.

- **Country Risk:** This risk refers to the possibility of experiencing losses or price fluctuations in a stock due to political or economic circumstances in the country where the stock market is located.

Many investors underestimate this risk because they perceive it as distant and unlikely. However, it is more common than it seems, and its effects can be devastating. Just look at what is happening in markets like Venezuela, Russia, or China, among others, to understand that the first decision an investor must make is to choose which country they want to invest in, as that will be where their money is deposited.

Focusing on market risk, what should we do to avoid the risk of incurring permanent capital losses? How should we manage this risk?

First and foremost, it's essential to understand that in any field, risk is closely linked to knowledge. The greater your understanding of a subject or action, the lower the risk you assume. This principle should always guide you. Therefore, be humble and honest with yourself. If you're unfamiliar with a stock, if you don't understand its business model, or its industry, recognize this and proceed accordingly. If you still want to invest in that stock, you must be able to comprehend the risks you are taking on.

I firmly believe that to achieve success in investing, it's important not to deceive yourself. Investing isn't about knowing more than your neighbor or coworker; it's about securing a satisfactory long-term return based on your goals, allowing you to sleep well despite market volatility. If you can achieve a good return by investing in businesses whose products you know thoroughly, like "The Coca-Cola Company" or "McDonald's," why invest in sectors you are unfamiliar with, such as biotechnology companies? Unless you are an expert in biotechnology, have family or friends who are, or possess insider information about a specific company because you know someone who works there, it's wise to steer clear of that sector. In investing, you won't earn any rewards for taking on high levels of difficulty, so set your ego aside and focus on making money in the most logical and straightforward way possible. This is my perspective, and it's what I strive to do every time I invest.

Once you know what you are doing, you can reduce or minimize market risk in various ways and methods. Some investors turn to complex instruments, such as financial derivatives or other hedging products. In my case, adhering to the previously mentioned philosophy of acting in the most logical and straightforward manner, I avoid engaging in complex financial instruments.

Another common practice for reducing investment risk is the use of a market order known as a "stop loss." This works as follows: once the investment is made, the investor sends an order to the broker to sell the entire position if the price of the stock reaches a certain level. For example, if I buy shares of Coca-Cola at $56 per share, I can then send a standing order to my broker to automatically sell all the shares I've acquired if the price drops to $50. In this way, I establish the maximum loss I am willing to accept and, therefore, limit the risk of my investment. I must confess that in my early days, I always used this order to limit potential losses. However, over the years, I have gained experience as an investor, which allows me to have greater confidence, knowledge, and conviction in my investments, so I no longer use the "stop loss" order. Nevertheless, it remains a useful tool for managing investment risk, especially for beginner investors.

Another way to limit risk is simply to invest a small amount of money, fully accepting the risk of permanent loss. This option is particularly interesting when looking to invest in high-growth stocks (typically technology sector stocks), whose prices are subject to high volatility. In these cases, a stock's price can drop by 60%, 80%, or even 90%, yet still provide spectacular long-term returns. For example, in 2000, during the burst of the so-called "dot-com bubble," Amazon, which at the time was a small disruptive company, saw its value plummet from $107 to $7.80 in less than a year, suffering a 92% decline. A drop of this magnitude triggers all "stop loss" orders, as most investors tend to use them to limit declines to 10%, 20%, 30%, or 40% of the purchase price. However, the investor who did not place any "stop loss" orders and had the courage to hold onto Amazon shares for 20 years ended up multiplying their investment by more than 450 times.

However, the vast majority of tech stocks or high-growth companies are not Amazon. Many of them fail in their attempts to become the next Amazon or Apple. For this reason, it is advisable to limit risk by investing a small amount of money and then observing how the business develops. In these cases, using a "stop loss" can prevent you from achieving excellent long-term returns.

Finally, it's worth noting that another common way to manage risk is through diversification. All capital managers, whether they are investment funds, pension funds, or hedge funds, use diversification to manage the risks of the investments they handle. Diversification is simply the logical consequence of the popular saying "don't put all your eggs in one basket" (because if the basket falls and breaks, you'll lose everything). You can diversify by acquiring different types of financial assets (stocks, bonds, mutual funds, ETFs, gold, etc.), purchasing stocks traded in various countries (for example, the U.S., Switzerland, Norway, Canada, etc.), holding strong and stable currencies that are not your local currency (such as U.S. dollars, Swiss francs, British pounds, etc.), or investing in stocks from different sectors or industries.

In conclusion, choose the method or system of risk management that you find most suitable or with which you feel most comfortable, but never forget to manage the risks of your investments. Sometimes, a complete disregard for risk management leads to permanent capital losses for beginner investors, pushing them to abandon the stock market altogether, which is a true tragedy.

Effective risk management is fundamental to achieving success in investing.

14. Psychology: Your Best Ally

"The investor's worst enemy is himself."

-Benjamin Graham-

If I tell you that success in investing largely depends on psychology, you might not believe me. I didn't either when I first started investing. I mistakenly thought that good returns in the stock market were reserved for brokers, financial analysts, and capital managers, as they all have advanced knowledge of finance. While it is indeed necessary to have financial knowledge to read and evaluate a company's financial statements—just as a doctor reads and assesses the results of a blood test—I believe that success in investing requires mastery of, or at the very least, a solid understanding of a discipline that has nothing to do with finance or numbers: human psychology.

The behavior of individuals when investing in the stock market has been the subject of numerous studies for decades, leading to the emergence of a new field in finance known as "behavioral finance." This discipline examines the mental biases that affect investors, as well as the distorted perceptions of reality that lead to irrational investment decisions.

The Efficient Market Hypothesis

In the 1970s, economist Eugene Fama developed the "efficient market theory," which essentially argues that the information and beliefs of market participants are fully reflected in stock prices, meaning their valuations are correct. The logical consequence of this theory is that no investor can consistently outperform the stock market, as all prices are accurately determined at any given moment. However, numerous market studies have shown that this theory is flawed, as investors often make decisions based on biases—and many times, irrationally. Furthermore, many investors and capital managers have consistently achieved returns higher than the overall market for decades. This demonstrates that human or social psychology plays a critical role in the valuation of financial assets.

Our emotions fluctuate daily, and we can swing from euphoria to depression in a short time. The way we perceive reality and the events around us is also not static. We are constantly exposed to an overwhelming number of influences (news, opinions, etc.), and our minds are not immune to them. Narratives shift, facts that once seemed clear become ambiguous or are viewed differently, causing our emotions to sway. The following chart illustrates the typical emotional cycle that any investor experiences:

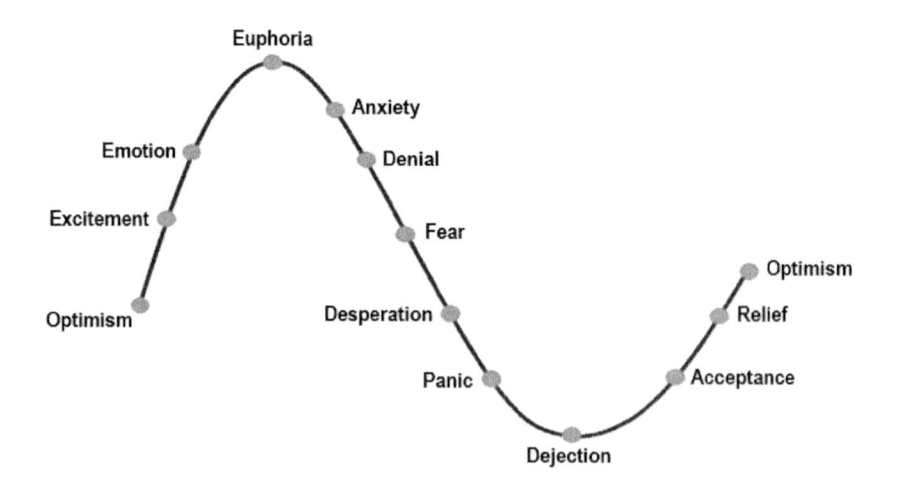

This chart, by itself, explains why so many people lose money investing in the stock market. You've probably guessed it by now, but let me confirm: the majority of investors buy stocks during times of excitement and euphoria and sell them when desperation and panic hit. In other words, they buy at 100, watch the stock rise to 140 (at the peak of euphoria), but ultimately sell it for 40, succumbing to the panic that grips the markets.

In contrast, the rational or intelligent investor is the one who not only avoids being influenced by the emotional swings of the market but also takes advantage of moments of widespread panic and desperation to acquire great businesses at bargain prices. Warren Buffett perfectly captured this mindset with his famous quote: "Be fearful when others are greedy, and be greedy when others are fearful."

Cognitive Biases

Below, I will outline some of the most common cognitive biases when investing, which can lead you to make poor decisions:

1) **Confirmation Bias:** This is the tendency to seek out specific and selective information that supports one's investment opinions, placing extra importance on that data. Conversely, facts or arguments that contradict these opinions are downplayed, allowing investors to reinforce the belief that their decisions are correct. This bias is very common and leads to a false sense of security.

2) **Anchoring Bias:** Anchoring refers to the tendency to stick to past information or fail to adjust an investment thesis to reflect the company's or market's new reality. Many investors remain fixated on their purchase price, even as they watch their investments lose value due to the company's or market's decline. This leads them to hold onto these investments, hoping the stock will recover, instead of reassessing their thesis and taking necessary action.

3) **Familiarity Bias:** Investors tend to perceive local, national, or nearby businesses as having lower risk, simply because of geographic proximity, or because the owners speak the same language or share the same nationality. This familiarity fosters a false sense of understanding about the business, leading to biased investment decisions.

4) **Overconfidence Bias:** This is the tendency to overestimate certain information or one's own investment abilities compared to others, often leading to risky decision-making.

5) **Disposition Effect:** This refers to the tendency of investors to sell assets that have increased in value while holding onto those that have decreased in value. The reason they don't realize their losses is that they don't want to admit the investment was unsuccessful.

6) **Representativeness Bias:** This is the tendency to make investment decisions based on stereotypes or prejudices, rather than analyzing the available data. For example, investing in luxury sector companies because one company in that sector (e.g., LVMH) has generated high returns in recent years.

7) **Loss Aversion:** Studies have shown that the pain from a loss is greater than the pleasure from a gain. This emotional imbalance explains the common tendency of investors to prefer avoiding losses over achieving gains.

As a result, it's crucial to understand the various cognitive biases that affect people when investing, for two main reasons. First, so you can identify market situations where widespread emotional imbalance is creating an excellent investment opportunity. Second, so you can recognize the biases that most influence you as an investor, allowing you to address, minimize, or even eliminate them.

By studying and analyzing your own psychology as an investor, as well as that of other market participants, you'll increase your chances of investment success. This self-awareness will also help you develop the mindset needed to navigate inevitable economic crises or stock market crashes, which I cover in the next chapter.

15. How to Handle a Stock Market "Crash"

One of the main reasons many people avoid the stock market is the fear of experiencing a stock market "crash" and potentially losing all or most of their money. There's a wealth of literature and urban legends surrounding stock market crises. It's a topic that generates significant media attention, even for those who have never invested in the stock market. However, understanding what triggers a stock market crash and knowing how markets have historically recovered after such crises is essential. This knowledge enables you to handle these situations differently from most people, whose perspective is often shaped by media bias.

So, what is a "crash" in the stock market? Essentially, a stock market crash is a sudden and steep decline in the valuations of financial assets. During a crash, the prices of stocks plummet due to thousands, or even millions, of sell orders executed within a short period. This massive wave of selling causes an imbalance between the supply and demand for shares. Sellers, overwhelmed by panic and desperation, are willing to lower their asking prices dramatically to find buyers and exit their investments.

There are many reasons why a stock market crash can occur. Some of the most common causes include:

- **Economic Recession**

    An economic recession is a period marked by a decline in the economic activity of a country or region, characterized by a decrease in GDP, an increase in unemployment, and a reduction in corporate profits. Typically, economic recessions tend to trigger a stock market crash due to economic uncertainty and low expectations regarding the future performance of business profits.

- **Media Coverage of Macroeconomic News**

When the media announces, for instance, that an economic recession or a political crisis is imminent, investors may lose confidence in the market and, as a result, sell their stocks at a faster-than-usual pace. This can lead to a sharp decline in stock prices. Interestingly, it is not even necessary for the predicted recession or political crisis to materialize; simply publicizing such news is often enough to cause most investors to flee the stock market.

- **Excessive Speculation**

Sometimes, investors buy trendy or popular assets simply to resell them in the short term at a higher price, taking advantage of the speculative frenzy. The buyer typically shares this same intent for immediate resale, and the cycle continues. These spirals of speculation regarding a particular asset lead to a significant increase in its valuation based on irrational future expectations—without regard for the underlying business's actual financial situation.

When an asset becomes overvalued, it is essential to keep in mind that, sooner or later, its price will adjust downward.

- **Wars or Terrorism**

Military conflicts and terrorism often undermine investor confidence and can consequently lead to a stock market crash.

- **Health Pandemic**

The outbreak of a health crisis (pandemic), like the one that occurred in 2020 with the coronavirus, creates chaos and panic among the population, which typically translates into a stock market crash.

When a stock market crash occurs, regardless of the cause behind it, it creates a situation of economic uncertainty and a loss of consumer confidence in the economy. This loss of confidence leads to a decline in prices, and this drop in prices further fuels investors' fears, spreading rapidly throughout the market. Additionally, companies that lose value during the stock market crash face greater difficulties in obtaining financing.

However, while it is true that some stock market crashes have had prolonged negative effects—such as the 1929 crash that triggered a severe economic downturn, known as the "Great Depression"—in most cases, stock market crashes have only produced short-term negative effects. Furthermore, history has shown us that when the market is depressed after a crash, it represents an excellent opportunity to invest. Let's look at some examples:

- **Crisis of 1956**

    In October 1956, there was a significant decline in stock markets worldwide, primarily caused by the Soviet Union's military intervention in Hungary and the escalating tension between the United States and the USSR during the Cold War. The markets experienced a correction of 21%. However, in the following years, the market returned to its valuation levels before the decline.

- **Crisis of 1962**

    The USSR installed nuclear missiles in Cuba, just 90 miles off the coast of Florida, to prevent the U.S. from invading the island. This led to heightened tensions between the two countries, and during this time, stock markets around the world experienced significant declines. This episode of the Cold War, known as the "Cuban Missile Crisis," resulted in a "flash crash," which is a rapid and significant drop in stock prices. The main U.S. stock index, the S&P 500, underwent a correction of 29%. Five years later, this index had appreciated by 112%.

- **Crisis of 1970**

An economic contraction occurred in the United States, which began in late 1969 and lasted until early 1971. The recession was primarily caused by rising inflation and commodity prices, such as oil, along with an increase in interest rates by the Federal Reserve. During this period, the S&P 500 experienced a decline of 32%. However, in the following five years, the index appreciated by 55%.

- **Crisis of 1973**

This crisis was mainly triggered by rising oil prices and inflation, which had a negative impact on the global economy and investor confidence. Additionally, the Yom Kippur War in October 1973 and the economic crisis in Europe also contributed to the market downturn. Stocks fell by 50%. However, in the five years that followed, the market rebounded by 111%.

- **Crisis of 1987**

October 19, 1987, is known as "Black Monday" due to the abrupt decline of stock markets worldwide that occurred on that day. This stock market crash was primarily caused by market volatility and a lack of investor confidence, leading to mass sell-offs. The market decline was exacerbated by the use of automated trading programs, which sold large quantities of shares as the market began to fall. The 1987 crisis was brief, lasting only a single day, but it generated a correction of 22.6% in the S&P 500. However, in the following five years, the index rebounded by 127%.

- **Crisis of 2000**

The crisis of 2000, also known as the "dot-com crisis," was an economic crisis caused by the collapse of technology companies lacking a strong business model. During the 1990s, tech companies related to a new technology—the internet—began to thrive. Many of these companies had no profits or solid business models, yet they received substantial investments due to market euphoria. When the market began to slow down at the end of the 1990s, many of these "dot-com" companies started to go bankrupt, provoking a stock market crash that began in March 2000 and lasted until October 2002. During this period, major American stock indices fell by 50%. Nevertheless, in the five years that followed, these same indices appreciated by 122%.

- **Crisis of 2008**

The financial and housing crisis of 2008 was a global economic crisis that began in 2007 with the collapse of subprime mortgages in the United States. The problem arose when many individuals who could not afford their subprime mortgages (mortgages offered to low-income individuals or those with high-risk profiles) began to default on their payments. This led to a crisis of confidence and liquidity in the global financial market, resulting in a sharp decline in property prices. During this period, the S&P 500 index fell by 57%, from peak to trough. But what happened in the following years? The same index appreciated by 207%.

- **Crisis of 2020**

    In March 2020, the COVID-19 pandemic, caused by the SARS-CoV-2 virus, triggered a global public health crisis. To curb the spread of the virus, many governments implemented social distancing measures and business closures. As a result, significant declines occurred in global stock indices. The S&P 500 fell by 34% in just one month. However, in the following year and a half, the index rebounded by more than 120%.

All stock market crises share a common element: stock indices have always recovered in the years immediately following the crisis. Regardless of the cause of the crisis or its duration, the stock market typically regains its previous level, on average, within a period of less than five years. However, before this recovery occurs, many investors have already sold their positions, usually during the downturn, influenced by widespread panic.

As a result, it is important for you as an investor to understand and accept the following:

1. All stock markets experience valuation adjustments for various reasons, and these adjustments can be so intense and sudden that they can lead to a sharp decline—often temporary—in stock prices. This is inevitable, and if you cannot withstand these periods of downward price adjustments or volatility, you are likely not ready to invest in the stock market.

2. After the storm comes the calm. Whatever correction is triggered by the stock market crisis, optimism begins to flourish again, and markets tend to recover over time. Consumers regain their confidence in the economy, investors regain their confidence in the markets, and the stock market begins to appreciate again, leaving the crisis episode behind. It has always been this way. We could find countless examples in the more than 200

years of stock market history, and nothing suggests that it will be different in the future.

3. During a stock market crash, it is important not to sell the securities in your portfolio without first conducting a thorough analysis of the business fundamentals and their potential evolution based on future expectations; otherwise, you could be giving away "gold." Additionally, it is recommended to closely observe market movements, as these periods of widespread pessimism often present very good investment opportunities.

16. Companies That Have Multiplied Their Wealth

The title of this book, "Multiply Your Wealth by Investing in Stocks", is neither a fallacy nor an exaggeration. By investing in companies through the purchase of shares in the stock market, anyone can potentially increase their wealth and multiply their initial investment capital several times over. Of course, this is not guaranteed—it's just a possibility, much like losses can also occur. But the simple fact that anyone has the chance to multiply their wealth, not due to luck—as happens with the lottery—but by making smart decisions, makes investing in companies truly exciting.

Below, I'll show you the trajectory of some companies that have multiplied in value, along with the gains their shareholders have made. Since there are thousands of companies whose stock values have soared, I've selected a few whose products or services are widely known to the public. This is to demonstrate that investing in them is not an unattainable dream limited to a handful of people with specialized knowledge. Any consumer could invest, or could have invested, in these companies with full awareness of what they are buying.

1. The Coca-Cola Company

'The Coca-Cola Company' is one of the most recognized and successful businesses worldwide in the beverage industry. Founded in 1886 by John Pemberton in Atlanta, Georgia, the company has experienced nearly unmatched growth and success throughout its history.

What started as a carbonated drink sold at a local pharmacy has grown into one of the most valuable and well-known brands in the world. The value of the "Coca-Cola" brand is immeasurable, and its ability to remain firmly embedded in the minds of consumers is a marketing triumph. The company has invested significant resources into building and promoting its brand, creating an identity that is associated with moments of happiness, friendship, and refreshment. Additionally, Coca-Cola has developed an extensive distribution network and forged strong relationships with retailers and strategic partners across the globe, ensuring its presence everywhere. Almost everyone knows this drink, and most people have tried it. You can find it in any bar, restaurant, or supermarket, and its success is undeniable. If you randomly asked 20 people who have never seen Coca-Cola's financial statements whether or not it's a successful company, I am confident the vast majority would say yes.

The following chart shows the performance of The Coca-Cola Company (Ticker: KO) stock over the past 30 years:

The Coca-Cola Company

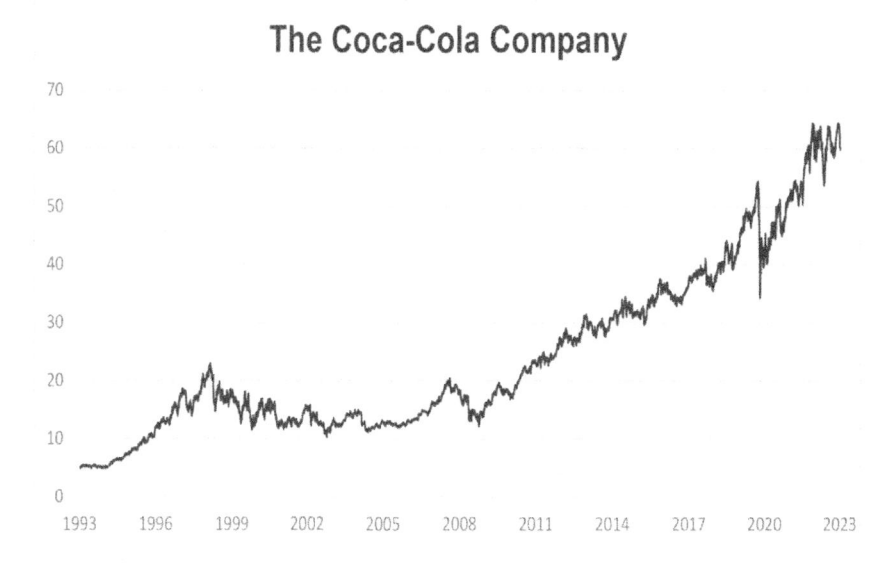

Period: 05/28/1993-05/28/2023.
Cumulative total return: 1,083.76%
Compound annual growth rate (CAGR): 8.59%

Let's imagine that an individual investor had invested $1,000 in Coca-Cola shares in May 1993. After 30 years, the market value of that investment would be $10,837.60. While it's true that the impact of inflation (the loss of purchasing power) should be considered in this amount, it's also important to note that Coca-Cola has distributed dividends throughout those 30 years. As a result, any investor who invested in Coca-Cola 10, 20, or 30 years ago would have multiplied the value of their investment several times over.

2. McDonald's Corporation

McDonald's is one of the largest and most recognized fast-food chains in the world. It was founded in 1940 by brothers Richard and Maurice McDonald in San Bernardino, California, USA. Initially, the restaurant focused on selling hamburgers, but over time, it expanded its product offerings to include chicken, fish, salads, and desserts.

The company's growth has been unstoppable, driven by several key factors. One of these is innovation. McDonald's introduced a new way of understanding dining, known as "fast food," which has been hugely successful with the public. Another factor is its franchise system, which has allowed McDonald's to expand rapidly and establish its brand globally at a relatively low cost.

McDonald's operates with impressive efficiency, able to handle large volumes of orders quickly. Additionally, it has adopted new technologies to further enhance this efficiency, such as self-service kiosks and online ordering. The company has also invested in automation in its kitchens, aiming to speed up service while maintaining quality.

Its logo and characters, like Ronald McDonald, have become globally recognized symbols, thanks to its effective marketing strategies.

The company's remarkable growth is also reflected in the performance of its stock:

McDonald's Corporation

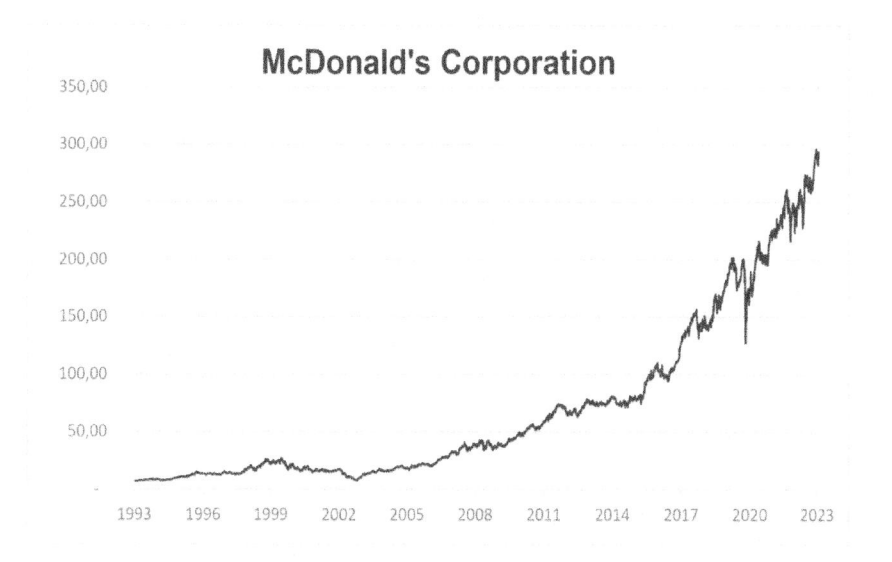

Period: 05/28/1993-05/28/2023.
Cumulative total return: 4,352%
Compound annual growth rate (CAGR): 13.49%

If you had invested $1,000 in McDonald's stock in May 1993, after 30 years, that investment would be worth $44,520. In other words, you would have multiplied your initial investment by more than 44 times.

Additionally, to calculate the total return on this investment, you would need to add the amounts received in dividends over the 30-year period.

3. LVMH

Louis Vuitton Moët Hennessy, commonly known as LVMH, is a French luxury goods conglomerate headquartered in Paris. It was founded in 1987 through the merger of two companies: Louis Vuitton and Moët Hennessy.

LVMH was established in 1854 as a company specializing in the manufacture of high-quality luggage and travel items. The brand became renowned for its exceptional craftsmanship and innovative designs.

On the other hand, Moët Hennessy was created in 1971 as a result of the merger of two champagne houses, Moët et Chandon and Hennessy, both recognized worldwide for their excellence in producing champagne and cognac, respectively.

Since 1987, LVMH has rapidly expanded across different segments of the luxury industry, including fashion, perfumes, cosmetics, watchmaking, and jewelry, by acquiring prestigious luxury brands. Iconic names such as Christian Dior, Givenchy, Fendi, Celine, Bulgari, Sephora, and TAG Heuer, among many others, have joined its portfolio. This inorganic growth has allowed LVMH to diversify its offerings and strengthen its position in the luxury goods market.

Thanks to its diversified portfolio of brands, all focused on excellence and craftsmanship, along with control over the value chain (production, distribution, marketing, and retail), and its global presence, LVMH has not only achieved significant growth but has also done so while generating a high return on invested capital. This reflects its pricing power and organizational efficiency.

The following graph illustrates how LVMH's stock has evolved from early

2005 to June 2023:

LVMH

Period: 01/03/2005-06/16/2023.
Cumulative total return: 1,435%
Compound annual growth rate (CAGR): 15.94%

The luxury goods sold by LVMH are globally recognized, and their success is no secret. Just look at the lines that form outside their stores. Thus, anyone had this investment opportunity right before their eyes. Anyone who invested in LVMH stock in early 2005 and remained patient over the next 18 and a half years would have multiplied their investment by more than 15 times. In other words, €1,000 invested at the beginning of 2005 would have grown to approximately €15,346, not including the returns generated from dividends during this 18-and-a-half-year period. It's truly remarkable for those who seized this opportunity.

4. Visa

Visa is a company that provides services related to the processing of electronic transactions and payments between merchants, financial institutions, and consumers. Since its founding in 1976, it has been a global leader in the electronic payment sector, forming an oligopoly alongside Mastercard.

This company has experienced substantial growth since its inception. It expanded its network of issuing banks worldwide, allowing Visa cards to be used beyond U.S. borders. This global network of issuers enables any Visa cardholder to make payments from anywhere in the world, making it very easy, convenient, and beneficial for users. This has been Visa's—and Mastercard's—significant competitive advantage over other competitors, as the global acceptance of their cards generates a network effect that is difficult to replicate.

Additionally, the company has reinvested a portion of its profits into enhancing technological infrastructure, which has ensured that payments are secure, fast, and reliable.

In the following chart, you can observe the performance of Visa stock over the past 15 years:

Visa

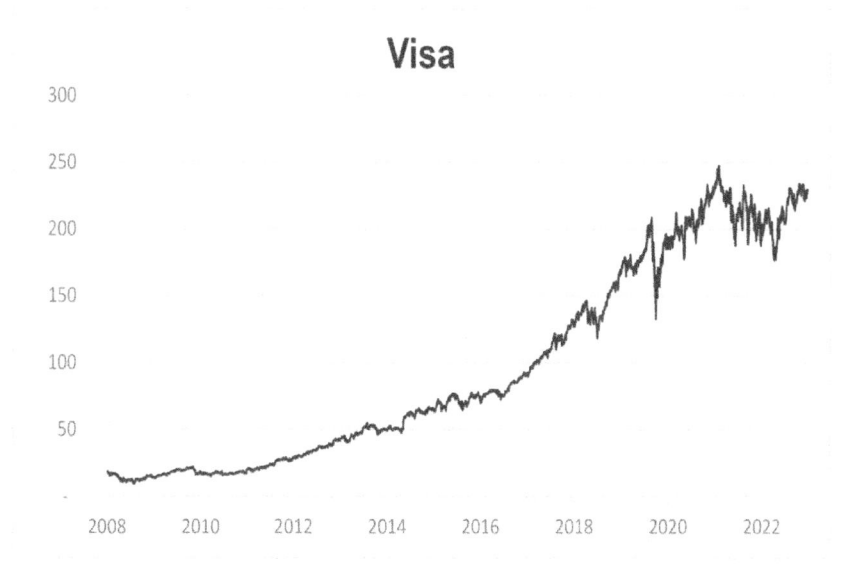

Period: 06/26/2008-06/23/2023
Cumulative total return: 1,189 %
Compound annual growth rate (CAGR): 18.58%

In June 2008, the stock was valued at $17.81. Fifteen years later, in June 2023, the stock traded at $229.55. The price of the stock multiplied by more than 11 times during this period. Who didn't know about Visa back in 2008? How many people in your circle were using a Visa card in 2008? Why didn't you buy a share of Visa back then?

5. Nike

Nike is one of the most recognized and successful brands in the world of sportswear and footwear. It was founded in 1964 by Bill Bowerman and Phil Knight under the name "Blue Ribbon Sports." Later, in 1971, Bowerman and Knight changed the company's name to Nike, in honor of the Greek goddess of victory.

Today, Nike is known worldwide and has a global presence. Its products are sold in numerous countries, supported by a wide distribution network that includes company-owned stores, retail outlets, and e-commerce platforms. Nike has managed to maintain its relevance and leadership in the sports footwear and apparel industry through constant innovation, effective marketing strategies, and a focus on the quality and performance of its products.

One of Nike's main competitive advantages is its strong emphasis on marketing and the creation of a powerful brand image. The company has invested heavily in advertising campaigns and has signed numerous famous athletes to promote its products. Sponsoring world-renowned athletes, such as Michael Jordan, helped the brand gain popularity and recognition.

Nike is a company that has adapted to market trends and demands and, over time, has diversified its product line to include sportswear, accessories, and equipment, in addition to footwear.

In the following graph, you can see how Nike's stock price has evolved over the last 30 years:

Nike

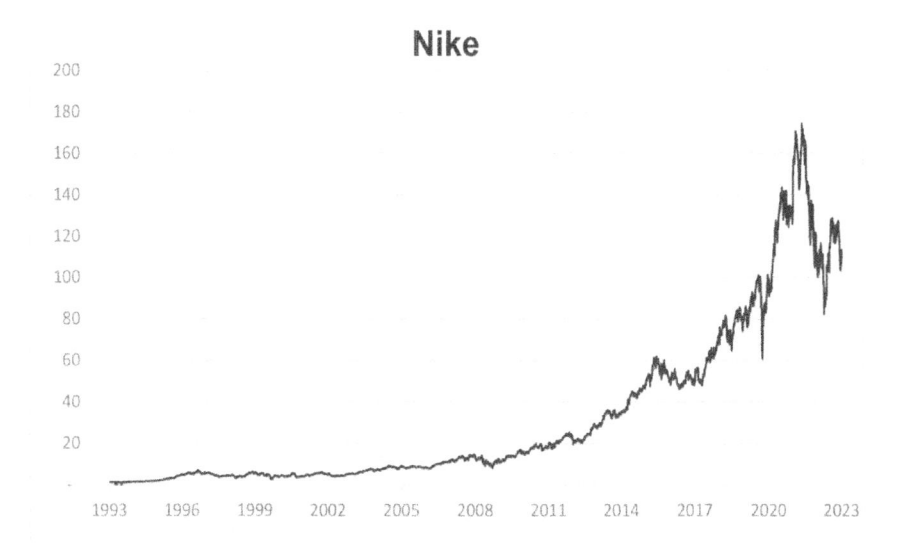

Period: 06/23/1993-06/23/2023
Cumulative total return: 9,141%
Compound annual growth rate (CAGR): 16.26%

I can't precisely determine how many pairs of Nike shoes I have bought over the last 30 years, but I'm sure it's quite a few. What would have happened if, instead of purchasing the shoes, I had bought shares of Nike? I would have multiplied my investment several times over. If I had purchased them in June 1993, I would have increased my investment by 91 times by June 2023. What an impressive return! Unfortunately, I didn't do that. And the worst part is that I was well aware of the quality and commercial success of their products, so I could have made that investment if I had possessed the knowledge I explain in this book.

6. Microsoft

Microsoft is one of the most recognized and successful technology companies in the world. It was founded by Bill Gates and Paul Allen in 1975, with its headquarters in Redmond, Washington, United States. Initially, the company focused on developing and selling the BASIC programming language for the Altair 8800 computers. However, it was with the launch of its operating system MS-DOS in 1981 that Microsoft began to experience significant growth.

The turning point for Microsoft came in 1985 when they launched Windows, a graphical operating system for PCs. Windows became the standard user interface for most personal computers, allowing Microsoft to solidify its position as a leader in the software market. As technology advanced, Microsoft continued to develop new versions of Windows, such as Windows 95, Windows XP, Windows 7, and the most recent version, Windows 10.

One of Microsoft's main competitive advantages is its wide range of products and services. In addition to the Windows operating systems, the company has developed productivity applications like Microsoft Office, which includes programs such as Word, Excel, PowerPoint, and Outlook. They have also ventured into the video game market with the Xbox console and offer cloud services through their Azure platform.

The Microsoft brand is widely recognized around the globe due to its international presence and impact on the technology industry. Its products and services are used by millions of people and businesses in various countries.

In the following chart, you can see how Microsoft's stock has performed over the last 30 years:

Microsoft

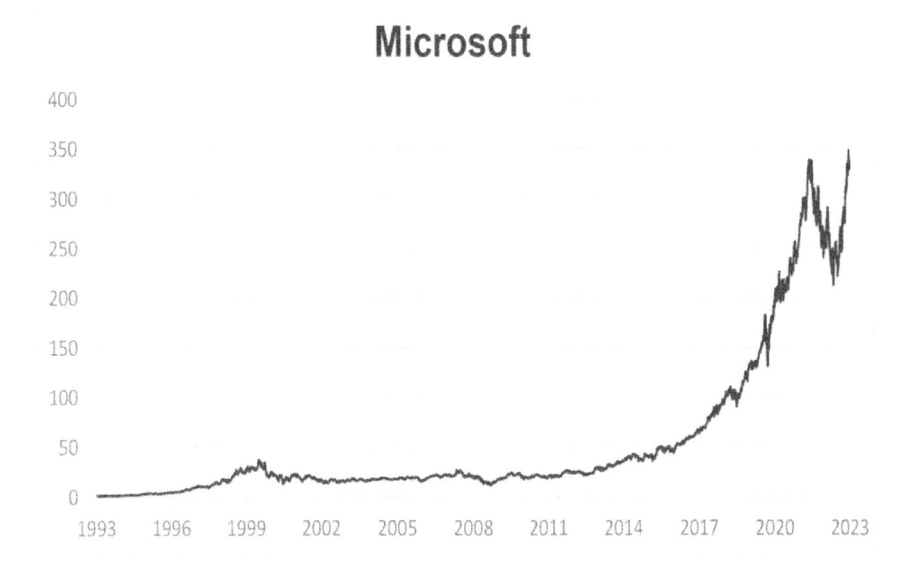

Period: 06/28/1993-06/28/2023
Cumulative total return: 18,924%
Compound annual growth rate (CAGR): 19.09%

Microsoft's stock experienced strong growth during the 1990s until the dot-com crisis erupted in 2000. In the following 10 to 12 years, the stock's performance was mediocre, despite the fact that the products and services offered by the company continued to enjoy the same level of popularity and success.

7. Monster Beverage

Monster Beverage is a company dedicated to the production and marketing of energy drinks. Founded in 1935 by Hubert Hansen and his wife, the company initially focused on producing and selling fruit juices and natural beverages. However, at the beginning of the 21st century, it underwent a transformation into what we now know as Monster Beverage.

The growth of Monster Beverage accelerated with the launch of its popular energy drink, "Monster Energy," in 2002. This beverage stood out due to its aggressive marketing and distinctive can design, allowing it to shine in the energy drink market. It became a phenomenon among younger, active consumers.

One of the reasons for the company's spectacular success is its specialized focus on the energy drink niche. While there are many competitors in the energy drink market, Monster has achieved a leadership position thanks to its ability to innovate and respond to consumer trends in this specific segment.

The stock price has seen significant growth over the past 20 years, in line with the company's business expansion. This growth is attributed to factors such as the global expansion of the brand, the introduction of new product lines, and the popularity of its flagship brand: Monster Energy.

Its specialized approach in the energy drink niche, along with its ability to innovate and adapt to market trends, are factors that have contributed to its current leadership position in the energy drink industry.

In the following graph, you can see the performance of Monster's stock over the past 17 years:

Monster Beverage

Period: 06/28/2006-06/28/2023
Cumulative total return: 1,472%
Compound annual growth rate (CAGR): 17.59%

In the long run, the stock price unequivocally reflects the performance of the underlying business, and this chart only confirms that. If you ever come across a chart like this, take the time to analyze the business, because without a doubt, you will be looking at a spectacular enterprise.

Equally spectacular are the other six businesses I have discussed in this chapter, as examples, since the list of companies that have been increasing their net worth for years or decades is extensive.

Final Thoughts

In the sixteen chapters of this book, I have aimed to explain, in a clear and straightforward manner, various concepts related to investing in real businesses through the purchase of stocks on a stock market. In my opinion, these are the most important lessons that anyone wishing to successfully start investing in stocks should learn. They are the basic guidelines that every investor should keep in mind. And believe me, knowing what is important and what is not when starting to invest can save you a lot of grief and money. I speak from personal experience.

However, keep in mind that the content of these sixteen chapters is merely an introduction. This book serves as an introduction to the stock market. If you truly want to delve into the world of investing, I encourage you not to stop reading (books, reports, letters published by fund managers, etc.).

That said, without a doubt, the best lessons you will learn—the ones that will leave an indelible mark on your mind—are the ones you will receive as an investor. And I don't mean investing in a simulator, but directly in the stock markets with your real money. The lessons you will learn from the market, primarily in the form of losses, will serve as an advanced masterclass. Typically, when someone loses money on an investment, they become determined to find the mistake they made. Once they identify it, they engrave it in their mind to avoid making it again.

I anticipate that you will make mistakes and experience losses, but this should not deter you from successfully investing in stocks, since investors around the world make mistakes and incur losses, even those who have multiplied their wealth several times. This is why it is important to manage risks, as I discussed in one of the chapters of this book, and to invest only a portion of your savings that is not necessary for your daily living expenses. Once, billionaire George Soros said, "It doesn't matter if you are right or wrong. What matters is how much you make when you're right and how much you lose when you're wrong." And that is truly the case. All investors make mistakes, so it is crucial to accept it, internalize it, and acknowledge that sooner or later, it will happen.

It is proven that the disappointment from a loss is greater than the joy from a gain. In other words, most investors prefer not to lose $100 than to gain $100. This bias leads many investors to miss out on good returns. By perceiving mistakes or losses as punishments, they let investment opportunities slip away out of fear or dread of that punishment. However, in my opinion, one should not view mistakes as penalties but as recurring events that provide valuable learning experiences. There are always significant lessons to be learned from losses, provided one is capable of sincere self-reflection and self-criticism. It is impossible not only to avoid mistakes but also to grow as an investor without having made them. This is why it is crucial to change your perception of mistakes as soon as possible and to learn from them, as they are what will help you improve as an investor. If you can learn from the mistakes made by others through reading, that's even better.

When you invest with your money (preferably not the money given to you by family members on your birthdays or Christmas, but the money you've earned through hard work), you will find that various emotions come into play. If the stock appreciates, you will feel joy and euphoria. Conversely, if the stock price declines, you will begin to feel fear or anxiety about losing your invested money, and doubts will arise that didn't occur before making the investment. It's the roller coaster that all investors face. Testing your emotions as an investor by investing with earned money is a necessary experience to begin learning.

Finally, I would like to conclude this final reflection by wishing you so much success as an investor. I hope the lessons included in this book contribute to that success, even if it's just by opening the door to concepts and ideas of great importance, no matter how simple they may seem at first.

If you wish to continue learning about investments, I recommend studying those who, in my opinion, are the greatest investors of all time:

- Benjamin Graham (considered the father of *"value investing"*).
- Warren Buffett (Berkshire Hathaway).
- Charlie Munger (Berkshire Hathaway).
- Peter Lynch (Magellan Fund).
- Terry Smith (Fundsmith).
- Stanley Drukenmiller (Duquesne Capital).
- Jim Simmons (Renaissance Technologies).
- François Rochon (Giverny Capital).

Thank You for Joining Me on This Journey!

If you've made it this far, I want to thank you for taking the time to read this book. I sincerely hope that what you've found within these pages has been helpful, interesting, or at least sparked new ideas for you.

Your opinion is very valuable. If you feel inclined to share it, you can leave a rating and/or review on Amazon. It would be warmly welcomed! You can easily do it by scanning the following QR code:

Once again, thank you. I wish you all the best on your journey as an investor. Who knows, perhaps we'll meet again in another reading!

Printed in Great Britain
by Amazon